Superstar Cars

Aston Martin

James Bow

🜪 Crabtree Publishing Company
www.crabtreebooks.com

Superstar Cars

Author: James Bow
Publishing plan research and development:
    Sean Charlebois, Reagan Miller
    Crabtree Publishing Company
Editors: Sonya Newland, Adrianna Morganelli
Proofreader: Molly Aloian
Editorial director: Kathy Middleton
Project coordinator and prepress technician: Ken Wright
Print coordinator: Katherine Berti
Series consultant: Petrina Gentile
Cover design: Ken Wright
Design: Paul Cherrill for Basement68
Photo research: Sonya Newland

Produced for Crabtree Publishing by
White-Thomson Publishing

Photographs:
Alamy: pbpgalleries: p. 8; AF archive: pp. 34-35;
ClassicStock: p. 40. **Corbis:** Hulton-Deutsch Collection: p. 10;
Sunset Boulevard: pp. 24-25. **Dreamstime:** Monkie: pp. 42-43;
Maxcortesiphoto: p. 54; Nomapu: pp. 54-55. **Getty Images:**
pp. 5, 15, 16; Popperfoto: p. 17; 2011 Bloomberg: p. 51. **iStock:**
Christopher Furlong: pp. 11, 52. **Motoring Picture Library:**
pp. 6-7, 9, 12-13, 18, 28-29, 30-31, 32-33, 36, 36-37, 38-39, 41.
Shutterstock: Fedor Selivanov: cover; Max Earey: pp. 1, 46-47,
48-49, 49, 56-57; dutourdumonde: pp. 4-5, 25, 26-27, 47; Adriano
Castelli: pp. 20, 22-23; m.bonotto: p. 23; aGinger: p. 26; Jose Gil:
pp. 44-45; Boykov: p. 50; testing: p. 53; lendy16: p. 57;
Fedor Selivanov: p. 58; esbobeldijk: pp. 58-59. **Topfoto:** Topham
Picturepoint: p. 19; **Wikipedia/Creative Commons License:**
dave_7: p. 14; thesupermat: pp. 20-21; Christopher Ziemnowicz:
p. 33; Jagvar: p. 43; Zölle: p. 45.

Library and Archives Canada Cataloguing in Publication

Bow, James, 1972-
        Aston Martin / James Bow.

(Superstar cars)
Includes index.
Issued also in electronic formats.
ISBN 978-0-7787-2099-7 (bound).--ISBN 978-0-7787-2104-8 (pbk.)

        1. Aston Martin automobile--Juvenile literature.
I. Title. II. Series: Superstar cars

TL215.A75B69 2012   j629.222'2   C2012-902281-0

Library of Congress Cataloging-in-Publication Data

CIP available at Library of Congress

Crabtree Publishing Company

www.crabtreebooks.com   1-800-387-7650

Printed in the U.S.A./052012/FA20120413

Published in Canada
Crabtree Publishing
616 Welland Ave.
St. Catharines, Ontario
L2M 5V6

Published in the United States
Crabtree Publishing
PMB 59051
350 Fifth Avenue, 59th Floor
New York, New York 10118

Published in the United Kingdom
Crabtree Publishing
Maritime House
Basin Road North, Hove
BN41 1WR

Published in Australia
Crabtree Publishing
3 Charles Street
Coburg North
VIC 3058

>> Contents

Chapter 1

►The Beginning of Elegance ►►►

Can a car share the image and character of the nation in which it was built so much that it becomes identified with that country? Many Italians take pride in Ferrari, a car whose design reflects the country's image of boldness and passion. Ford's Mustang waves the U.S. flag and speaks to America's love of the open road. For many, Aston Martin is a very British automobile.

Symbol of Britain

There is a reason why Britain's most famous fictional super spy, James Bond, drives an Aston Martin. They are among the most luxurious cars that you can buy, but they are understated and elegant. They pamper the driver, but the smooth curves cover a core of steel. It is easy to forget that Aston Martins are also some of the fastest cars on the racetrack, with a **pedigree** that stretches back to the early days of car production in the UK.

Aston Martins have represented classic British style and elegance for nearly 100 years.

Early beginnings

The story of Aston Martin begins in 1905, when an Englishman named Lionel Martin met the mechanical engineer Robert Bamford at a cycling club. This was just 30 years after Karl Benz had built his first *Motorwagen*. The assembly line had not yet been invented, and the cars of the day were often handmade—sometimes using bicycle parts!

Going it alone

Bamford believed he could build a better car than any available at the time. And, with Martin's backing, he did just that. Using a **modified** Singer sports car, Martin and Bamford tested their skills on a number of trial races and hill climbs around the UK. At first, they partnered with the Singer automobile company, selling Singer's cars. As their knowledge grew, however, the two men decided to build and sell their own cars. They founded Bamford & Martin Limited in June 1913.

Lionel Martin at the wheel of his Aston Martin at Brooklands racing circuit.

Lionel Martin

Lionel Martin was born in Cornwall, England, in 1878. His father was very wealthy, so Lionel could support himself while building and racing cars. Lionel's lifestyle was expensive and his business interests put him in debt, but with luck and with friends, he was never poor. After leaving Aston Martin in 1926, he spent his time building and riding bicycles. He died in a cycling accident in 1945.

Interruptions

Lionel Martin's business was a labor of love. There were bigger and better-financed car companies already in operation, including Singer, Rolls Royce, and Daimler. But Martin was determined.

The first car that bore the Aston Martin name had a **chassis** made by the Italian company Isotta Fraschini and a four-cylinder engine by the British manufacturer Coventry-Simplex.

The car rolled off the line in March 1915, but World War I stopped production there. Britain needed weapons, and manufacturing space could not be wasted on luxuries like sports vehicles. Martin and Bamford sold their machinery to the Sopwith Aviation Company and joined the war directly. Martin fought in the Royal Navy and Bamford joined the army.

Beginning again

After the war, Martin and Bamford bought factory space on Abingdon Road in Kensington, and were soon putting Aston Martin cars through their paces. The first was built using a Coventry-Simplex engine and a three-speed **transmission**. The brakes worked on the rear wheels only. This **prototype** came to be known as the Coal Scuttle because of its simple, gray, two-seater body. Although the engine was outdated, Martin and his workers entered it in the London-Edinburgh Trial in June 1919—and won a gold medal.

A 1921 Aston Martin competes in a dusty hill climb, watched by a crowd of fascinated spectators.

What's in a name?

With Robert Bamford providing mechanical skill and Lionel Martin supplying both skill *and* money, Martin decided he had earned the right to name the new company after himself. The "Aston" came from the village of Aston Clinton, in the English county of Buckinghamshire. The village hosted a hill climb up nearby Aston Hill, where Martin and Bamford's cars did very well. A plaque now marks the site.

6

Making an impression

The next prototype, built in 1921, would be the basis of Martin's first **production cars**. With its side-valve engine, four-speed gearbox, and more elegant style of body—as well as better wheels and front-wheel brakes—the model impressed critics. This car was raced at the famous Brooklands circuit in May 1921, where it won with an average speed of 69.75 mph (112.23 km/h). The model was available to the public for an expensive £850 (around US$1,300).

AMAZING FACTS

Behind every great man

Lionel Martin's wife, Katherine, is not often mentioned in the history of Aston Martin, but she was a savvy businesswoman in her own right. In the early 1920s, she assisted her husband on the board of the company and helped steer it to its early success.

Green Pea, Razor Blade, and Halford Special

At the same time, Bamford and Martin produced three team cars specifically for racing, using 16-valve twin-cam engines. The first of these was chassis 1914, nicknamed the "Green Pea," which was raced in the French Grand Prix in 1922.

Chassis 1915, known as the "Razor Blade," had a 1.5-liter engine capable of 55 **brake horsepower (bhp)** at 4200 rpm. It was designed to be as light and **aerodynamic** as possible, and built to break the record for the fastest average speed over a whole hour, which was 101.39 mph (163.17 km/h) at the time. However, while it looped the track at Brooklands at speeds well over 100 mph (160 km/h), troubles with the car's tires forced Martin to abandon the record attempt.

Vital Statistics

Standard Sports Series

Production years: 1921–25
No. built: 55
Top speed: 104 mph (166 km/h)
Engine type: 16-valve twin-cam
Engine size: 1.5 liters, 55 bhp at 4200 rpm
Cylinders: 4
Transmission: N/A
CO$_2$ emissions: N/A
EPA fuel economy ratings: N/A
Price: Approx. US$1,300 (£850)

Chassis 1916 was Aston Martin's first customer car. It was built for a racecar driver, who crashed it in 1924 and later sold it to Major Frank Halford. Halford rebuilt the car, which ended up bearing the name "The Halford Special."

■■▶
In the 1980s, the first Razor Blade was bought and restored by a private owner.

Racing driver Count Zborowski invested money in Aston Martin, and competed for the company in the 1923 French Grand Prix.

Going broke

Lionel Martin raced for records and **prestige**, so only 55 of the Standard Sports series were built for sale. Although the company had acquired a reputation for building fast and durable vehicles, Bamford and Martin still struggled financially. Martin bought out Bamford's stake in 1922, and got funding from the wealthy Count Louis Zborowski. Even this could not save the company, and in 1924 it declared **bankruptcy**. Martin had discovered that it was one thing to build a new car company; it was quite another to keep it running.

Where are they now?

The Green Pea was bought by a collector in 1958. The Razor Blade was raced well into the 1950s, before being sold to the National Automobile Museum in the U.S.A., and then bought by a private collector. The current owner of the Halford Special bought what was left of the car in the 1970s, located the original parts, and restored it.

9

Chapter 2

Life After the Founder Leaves »

In the early 1920s, Lionel Martin had realized his dream. His cars had raced at Brooklands and in the Grand Prix. He had made a name for himself as a maker of fast, high-quality racing vehicles. But although Martin counted some of the richest people in England among his customers, many were also his friends and Martin did not want to take advantage of them for his own profit.

The end for Lionel Martin

Martin was not charging as much as he could for his vehicles. Despite investments by a variety of **patrons**, the company went bankrupt. Finally, the Abingdon Road factory closed in 1926 and Lionel Martin walked away.

The "Buzzbox"

This was not the end for Aston Martin, though. In 1926, two skilled engineers and mechanics named Bill Renwick and Augustus "Bert" Bertelli developed an overhead-cam, four-cylinder engine, using a new combustion chamber design.

They called it the "Buzzbox," and they built a car using it. But they knew they needed a famous name to help them market their design.

A woman inspects Renwick's and Bertelli's engine in an Aston Martin at the 1929 Motor Show at Olympia, in London.

Aston Martin reborn

The two men were contacted by Lady Charnwood, an aristocrat named Dorothea Thorpe who had bought out Lionel Martin. With Renwick's and Bertelli's powerful new engine, Aston Martin's good name, and money from Lady Charnwood's investors, the company began to rise from the ashes. The new Aston Martin Motors Limited was incorporated on October 12, 1926, with Renwick, Bertelli, and John Benson (Lady Charnwood's son) as directors.

Changing logo

The first Aston Martin logo appeared in 1920. It featured a circle containing the letters A and M. This logo served the company until 1932, when the first wings were added—signifying speed. Over time, the wings have become less swept back and more stylized. The current version dates from 1987, and adds a splash of green around the company name.

 The current Aston Martin logo was introduced in 1987.

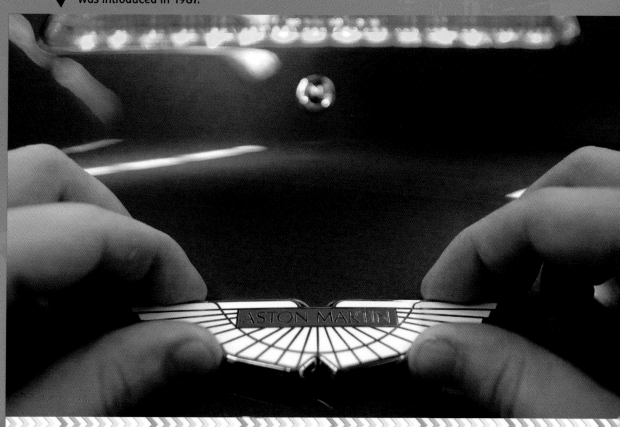

The Bertelli cars

Production moved to the former Whitehead Aircraft Ltd. works in Feltham. As Aston Martin's new technical director, Bertelli designed and produced the company's famous "Bertelli" cars, including the First Series, Aston Martin International, the International Le Mans, the Mark II, and the 15/98. These cars had 1.5- or two-liter engines and were mostly open-topped, two-seater sports cars, although a limited number of four-seater "tourers" were also produced. Bertelli's brother, Enrico Bertelli, built many of the cars' bodies.

■■➡

With its 1.5-liter, 16-valve twin-cam engine, Bertelli's Le Mans series could reach speeds of 81 mph (130 km/h).

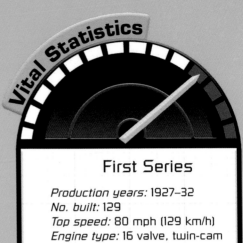

Vital Statistics

First Series

Production years: 1927–32
No. built: 129
Top speed: 80 mph (129 km/h)
Engine type: 16 valve, twin-cam
Engine size: 1.5 liters, 56 bhp at 4200 rpm
Cylinders: 4
Transmission: N/A
CO_2 emissions: N/A
EPA fuel economy ratings: N/A
Price: N/A

Facing the Depression

Bertelli's designs proved popular among Britain's wealthy classes. The company was doing well. However, in 1929 the world economy crashed and the **Great Depression** began. People lost their fortunes and could no longer afford luxury cars. By 1932, Aston Martin faced bankruptcy once again.

Financial difficulties had already forced Charnwood and Renwick to leave, so Bertelli sought help from Gordon Sutherland, who had just graduated from college with a degree in automobile engineering. Sutherland convinced his wealthy father to buy out Aston Martin and make him joint managing director with Bertelli.

Le Mans Mark II

In 1934, Aston Martin introduced the Le Mans Mark II. This vehicle boasted a modified **cylinder head** and a new oil filter that allowed the engine to produce 70 bhp at 5200 rpm. Taking on the Tourist Trophy—a 478-mile (769-km) race—the Aston Martin finished third, with an average speed over six hours of 74.53 mph (119.92 km/h).

"Bert" Bertelli

Born in Wales to Italian parents, Bertelli moved to Italy early in his career to work with Fiat, but later returned, reportedly because his favorite sport, soccer, could not be played on Sundays in Italy. Bertelli was a gifted engineer and mechanic, and liked to race the cars he built. His work at Aston Martin allowed him to build excellent racing models. He left the company when it quit racing in 1936.

The Ulsters

Aston Martin topped the Mark II with the performance of three cars known as the "Ulsters." With their 1.5-liter engines boosted to 80 bhp, the cars had a top speed of 102 mph (164 km/h). They dominated the races in 1934, including taking first, second, and third place during the British Tourist Trophy race at Goodwood.

In spite of these successes, by 1936 Aston Martin was back on shaky ground, and Bertelli chose to leave the company to Gordon Sutherland. Sutherland decided to stop racing and concentrate on the production of road cars. Once again, the small scale of production damaged the company. By 1939, only 700 cars had been made—not enough to keep Aston Martin afloat. To add to the problems, Britain was once again on the brink of war.

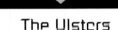

Vital Statistics

The Ulsters

Production years: 1934–36
No. built: 21
Top speed: 102 mph (164 km/h)
Engine type: Inline 4 with dry sump
Engine size: 1.5 liters, 80 bhp at 5250 rpm
Cylinders: 4
Transmission: 4-speed manual
CO_2 emissions: N/A
EPA fuel economy ratings: N/A
Price: N/A

Aston Martin's success with the Ulsters led the company to produce replicas of the lightweight two-seater. A total of 21 cars were produced, all of which are in private hands today.

Off to war again

In September 1939, tensions that had been building throughout Europe erupted into fighting. Germany invaded Poland, and Britain declared war in response. World War II had begun. Aston Martin had barely survived the Depression, but now it would have to shut down. The country needed its factories to build weapons again. The company's Feltham plant went back to producing aircraft components. New cars would have to wait until the fighting stopped.

Racing driver J. L. Donkin crawls out of his Aston Martin after skidding at the Ards circuit in Belfast, Northern Ireland, in 1935.

Endurance races

In the early days of auto racing, many races were more about endurance than speed. Courses tested both the drivers' stamina and the skill of their crews, who would have to make on-the-spot repairs. Just finishing a race was an achievement. At the Spa 24-Hour race in Belgium in July 1936, Aston Martin was awarded the Liedekerke Challenge Cup for "most meritorious performance by an entry that failed to finish."

Chapter 3

Aston Martin Makes Its Name

Throughout the war, Aston Martin's plant in Feltham built aircraft components, but one engineer in the company was not willing to let go of his fascination with cars. Claude Hill had been with the company since Bertelli took over. During his spare time—and using rare spare parts—he built a prototype of a sports sedan car in a neglected corner of the plant. He called this car the Atom.

After the war

World War II ended in 1945, but Aston Martin did not restart automobile production right away. Britain was busy rebuilding its bombed-out cities, and supplies and labor were limited for something as "frivolous" as luxury sports cars. In addition to this, Aston Martin's machinery was worn out and needed replacing.

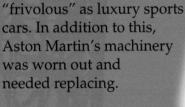

The Atom was Claude Hill's pet project, but it was this sedan that attracted David Brown to Aston Martin and started a whole new era for the company.

Car company for sale

Gordon Sutherland knew he needed a major investment in order to get Aston Martin up and running again, but money was scarce.

Admitting defeat, he placed an advertisement in the *London Times*, offering "Sports Car Company for Sale" and asking for £30,000 (US$121,000). A tractor-maker named David Brown saw the ad and traveled to Feltham to look over the factory. There, he spotted Claude Hill's Atom and asked to drive it. He fell in love with the car and, after some negotiation, bought Aston Martin for £20,500 (US$823,000).

Brown in gear

David Brown started work in his family's gear-making business, and by 1931 he was managing director. He branched out into tractors in 1939, making them in his factory throughout World War II. By the end of the war, over 7,000 units had been sold—and Brown was a wealthy man. His love of fast cars led him to buy Aston Martin in 1947, and he led the company to build its most *iconic* vehicles.

■ In his spare time, Brown (pictured right) owned racehorses and liked to play polo. He raced cars and motorcycles and could fly planes.

Bringing in Lagonda

Even with David Brown at the helm, the revitalized company did not get off to a flying start. Financial and labor shortages continued. To help get things moving, Brown looked around for a partner company, and eventually bought rival automaker Lagonda. Together, the two companies had the resources to get down to business.

From 1919 until 1932, Bentley owned his own auto company, which was later bought out by Rolls Royce.

The Spa Replica

In 1948, Aston Martin put Claude Hill's Atom engine to the test in the Spa 24-Hour race. The car took first place. It was quickly rebuilt as the "Spa Replica," and debuted at the 1948 London Motor Show. With its high price tag, though, there were few interested buyers. But David Brown would lend his initials to a new production line of Aston Martin/Lagonda cars that ended up becoming the company's most famous creations, starting with the DB1.

Lagonda and Bentley

Lagonda was founded in 1906 by Wilbur Gunn, a Scotsman who built and raced motorcycles before moving onto cars. His first car, a 20-hp, six-cylinder Torpedo, won the Moscow-St Petersburg Trial in 1910. Between the wars, Lagonda produced luxury sports cars. In the 1940s, Lagonda's greatest asset was Walter Owen Bentley, who helped the company develop its first postwar cars.

The birth of the DBs

Also debuting at the London Motor Show was a less expensive production car that later became known as the DB1. This boasted a two-liter, four-cylinder, 90-**horsepower (hp)** engine developed by Claude Hill. The engine sat in a modern two-seater **roadster** body, and it could propel the car to speeds of 93 mph (150 km/h). Although only 13 production DB1s were built, it proved a good learning experience for when Brown and his engineers upgraded the line with the DB2.

The DB1 was considered overweight and underpowered, and only 13 production versions were built.

THX 231

ASTON MARTIN 2 LITRE SPORTS MODEL

⟫ DB Mark IIs at Le Mans

Three DB Mark II prototypes were entered into Le Mans in 1949. These had a shorter **wheelbase**, a lighter tubular chassis, and a **streamlined** body. Two of them used Claude Hill's four-cylinder engine, while the third had a more powerful six-cylinder, 2.6-liter, twin overhead-cam engine developed under the supervision of Lagonda's W. O. Bentley. At Le Mans, one of the cars placed seventh overall and third in its class.

This was successful enough for David Brown to introduce the new six-cylinder DB2 at the 1950 New York Motor Show. The attractive design and the model's success at the 1950 Le Mans race turned heads, and the company found that it could not make the cars fast enough to meet demand. By 1953, 411 DB2s had been built.

A car of distinction

The Aston Martin DB2 sales brochure claimed: "The DB2 is a car of distinction, luxuriously appointed and immaculately finished. Worthy successor to 30 years of Aston Martin winners at Spa, Ulster and Le Mans, the DB2 has already claimed a formidable lead among today's best fast cars."

■ Built between 1950 and 1952, the
▬ DB2 had a water-cooled, cast-iron,
↓ inline-6 engine and a top speed of 110 mph (177 km/h).

DB2/4

The DB2/4 went into production in 1953 as the first 2+2 seater. In 1954, Brown bought the Tickford coachbuilding company and within a year, all of Aston Martin's operations had moved to the Tickford plant in Newport Pagnell. There, work began on the Mark II model of the DB2/4.

Before the move to Newport Pagnell, the DB2/4 was a **grand tourer**, available as a drophead **coupe** or as a 2+2 hatch-back. Aston Martin originally used the same 125-hp engine as the DB2, but later replaced this with a 2.9-liter engine capable of 140 hp and top speeds of 120 mph (193 km/h). They sold 565 of these cars.

A body for the car

The talent brought in from the Tickford coachbuilding company added tailfins, bubble-type taillights, and chrome to the Mark II version of the DB2/4. The car looked sleeker and faster, and in fact it *was* faster, because the changes on the inside included a high-compression engine capable of 165 hp. Only 199 Mark IIs were made, but Aston Martin was already preparing for the DB Mark III.

Faster than the original DB2, the DB2/4 could go from 0 to 60 mph in 12.6 seconds.

Vital Statistics

DB2/4

Production years: 1953–57
No. built: 764
Top speed: 120 mph (193 km/h)
Engine type: Inline 6
Engine size: 2.58 liters, 125 bhp at 5000 rpm
Cylinders: 6
Transmission: 4-speed manual
CO$_2$ emissions: N/A
EPA fuel economy ratings: 17 mpg (14 l/100 km)
Price: US$13,900

DB Mark III

The DB Mark III was built around Bentley's Lagonda 2.9-liter straight-6 engine. Using twin **carburetors** and a dual exhaust system, the car was capable of 178 hp, had an **acceleration** of 0–60 mph (97 km/h) in 9.3 seconds, and a top speed of 120 mph (193 km/h). Variants increased the engine's power to 195 hp. One of them, fitted with a racing engine, reached 214 hp.

The Mark III also boasted a redesigned instrument panel, a hatchback body with fold-down rear seats, and smoother, sleeker curves. In 1959, the magazine *Road & Track* praised the vehicle, calling it, "a car for connoisseurs" with "many virtues and few faults."

DB Mark III

Production years: 1957–59
No. built: 551
Top speed: 120 mph (193 km/h)
Engine type: Straight-6 with twin SU carburetors
Engine size: 2.9 liters, 178 hp
Cylinders: 6
Transmission: N/A
CO_2 emissions: N/A
EPA fuel economy ratings: N/A
Price: US$7,450

By 1959, Aston Martin had built and sold 551 DB Mark IIIs.

The DB3

Aston Martin also produced the DB3—a slab-sided evolution on the DB2 that was designed to win races. The first vehicles were too heavy to challenge the front runners, but the DB3S, with a lighter chassis, shorter and narrower wheelbase, and stronger engine (a straight-6, 2.9-liter capable of 237 hp), saw greater success.

With its curves and strong arches over the wheel, the DB3 was designed to look good – and move fast.

The car's shape not only gave it a striking appearance, it also added stability and helped deflect hot air from the engine, releasing it behind the front wheels.

The Mark III's success on the road and racetrack was not what assured its immortality, however. That came through a stroke of luck, as Aston Martin's work impressed a popular author of the day.

AMAZING FACTS

Mark III records

The racing DB3S started in 35 major races during its lifetime—and won 15 of them. Its successor, the DBR1, won the 1959 Le Mans race outright, and took the title of World Sportscar that year.

Chapter 4

Bond's Car ⟫⟫ ⟫⟫ ⟫⟫

In 1959, a British author named Ian Fleming published *Goldfinger*, the fifth book in the series following the adventures of British super spy, James Bond. In the book, Bond drives a secret service-issued Aston Martin DB Mark III, trailing the villain Goldfinger from England to Switzerland.

A spy's choice

Fleming was already famous for his popular novels, which drew on his own experiences as a spy during World War II. In the book, he described Bond's car ride at length, and soon the Aston Martin became known among the public as "Bond's Car."

David Brown encouraged the Bond connection. When *Goldfinger* was made into a movie in 1964, Bond's car was upgraded to an Aston Martin DB5. The film was so successful that it not only assured Bond's place in popular culture, it also made Aston Martin cars an iconic symbol of the genre, and of Britain.

Sean Connery as Bond, with his now-iconic Aston Martin, on the set of *Goldfinger*.

BMT 216A

More movies

Aston Martins appeared in a number of Bond films, including *Thunderball*, *GoldenEye*, and *Tomorrow Never Dies*. More recently, in *Casino Royale* (2006), Bond wins his silver DB5 in a poker game, and gets an Aston Martin DBS as his company car. The connection has been parodied in other films, including the Pixar film *Cars 2*, where the spy character Finn McMissile is an Aston Martin.

The DB4 was capable of 240 hp, with a high gear ratio that pushed the car to speeds of up to 139.3 mph (224.2 km/h).

Surging ahead

With this success under his belt, David Brown pushed for a redesign for Aston Martin's DB4 model. The car offered a new 3.7-liter engine with a dual-cam overhead straight-6, and the cylinder head and block built from lighter aluminum. It could go from 0 to 60 in 9.3 seconds and could do 14.7 miles to a gallon of fuel. A lightweight tube-frame body was designed by Carrozzeria Touring of Milan, Italy, which gave the car a "continental" look that surprised critics at the 1958 London Motor Show. A racing version of the car, the DB119/1 prototype, won the BRDC GT (later the British GT) race at Silverstone on May 2, 1959.

AMAZING FACTS

DB4 success

The DB4 was Aston Martin's most popular model yet, with 1,210 cars produced. Racing versions of the DB4 GT won at Nassau, Brands Hatch, Monza, and Bonneville, before Brown retired Aston Martin from racing to concentrate on road cars.

>> The DB5

In 1963, Aston Martin took the last series of the DB4 (the Vantage), and upgraded it into the DB5. This was the car that assured Aston Martin's immortality. The DB5's appearance in the James Bond movie *Goldfinger* gave Aston Martin loads of publicity, and has been called "the greatest act of product placement in movie history." Aston Martin loaned the movie producers prototype cars of the DB5, so the cost to the company was very low.

The DB5 and the DB4 Series 5 Vantage looked very alike—both had an elegant body designed by Carrozzeria Touring. Beneath the hood, however, the DB5 boasted a four-liter straight-6 engine capable of 282 hp, and a five-speed ZF gearbox. A standard DB5 could reach 114 mph (231 km/h), with models upgraded using triple Weber carburetors capable of 150 mph (240 km/h).

Vital Statistics

DB5

Production years: 1963–65
No. built: 983
Top speed: 145 mph (233 km/h)
Engine type: All-aluminum inline-6
Engine size: 4 liters, 282 hp at 5500 rpm
Cylinders: 6
Transmission: ZF 5-speed *synchro-mesh* (manual or automatic)
CO_2 emissions: N/A
EPA fuel economy ratings: 14.7 mpg (16 l/100 km)
Price: Approx. US$6,600 (£4,248)

After *Goldfinger*, the silver DB5 reappeared in *GoldenEye* (1995) and *Tomorrow Never Dies* (1997) as James Bond's personal car.

The DB6

For the next series, Aston Martin took the design of the DB6 back in-house, building around the DB5 look and chassis. The company raised the roofline to improve headroom, lengthened the wheelbase for improved stability and legroom, and offered the option of power steering and air conditioning. In terms of power, the DB6 offered only modest improvements on the performance of the top-of-the-line DB5, which led some critics to call the design "dated."

Vital Statistics

DB6

Production years: 1965–71
No. built: 1,967
Top speed: 150 mph (241 km/h)
Engine type: All-aluminum inline-6
Engine size: 4 liters, 282 hp at 5500 rpm
Cylinders: 6
Transmission: ZF 5-speed manual or Borg-Warner 3-speed automatic
CO_2 emissions: N/A
EPA fuel economy ratings: N/A
Price: Approx. US$7,800 (£4,998)

The DB6 was unveiled at the 1965 London Motor Show and continued in production until 1971.

The DBS

As the DB6 was being introduced, Aston Martin also unveiled the DBS, a larger coupe with four full-sized seats, bearing the same engine as the smaller model. It also had a more modern look, thanks to designer William Towns. This featured a squared-off front grille, which was unusual compared to Aston Martin's traditional curves, but very much in fashion with other cars of the day. Other Aston Martin features were retained, including a hood air scoop, wire spoke wheels, and side air-vents. Exactly 787 DBSs were produced until the line was retired in 1972, including the DBS V8, released in 1969.

Brown's heyday

David Brown had led Aston Martin for over two decades, establishing the company's reputation as a builder of high-quality luxury automobiles. The car was part of the popular culture of Britain, and well known to Americans. Models were appearing in movies, and hundreds were being sold in showrooms on both sides of the Atlantic. In terms of its image, the company had never been stronger.

Vital Statistics

DBS

Production years: 1967–72
No. built: 787
Top speed: 140 mph (225 km/h)
Engine type: All-aluminum inline-6
Engine size: 4 liters, 283 hp at 5500 rpm
Cylinders: 6
Transmission: ZF 5-speed manual or Borg Warner automatic
CO_2 *emissions:* N/A
EPA fuel economy ratings: N/A
Price: Approx. US$6,960 (£4,473)

The DBS took the Aston Martin look in a new direction, with a fashionable square front grille.

Into the 1970s

However, Aston Martin was still on financially shaky ground. Building automobiles in the UK—especially ones as high-quality as those Aston Martin produced—was expensive, and greatly affected by fickle demand. At the start of the 1970s, the British economy weakened.

A sharp increase in oil prices and labor troubles in the country pushed Aston Martin into financial difficulties. Finally, in 1972—after 25 years of being in charge of the company—David Brown decided it was time to move on. He put Aston Martin up for sale.

Chapter 5
A Change of Ownership ⟫⟫⟫⟩

The first new owner was a holding company called Company Developments Ltd., run by a chartered accountant named William Willson. Financial problems increased, though, and Aston Martin declared bankruptcy in 1975, before being sold to two North American businessmen named Peter Sprague and George Minden. Unlike Willson, Sprague and Minden were interested in building cars, and they launched a turnaround strategy. Fortunately, they had a strong model on which to rebuild the company.

Brown's parting gift

Although he had sold his interest in the company, David Brown had not left Aston Martin in the lurch. At the time of his departure, the Aston Martin DBS was the **flagship** of the company. The car came in two versions—a standard model containing a V6 engine, and the DBS V8, with a much more powerful V8 engine.

The V8 was more popular and sold for much more money. In 1972, the V6 model was dropped and the eight-cylinder DBS became the Aston Martin V8. It would be the main model built by the company for the next two decades.

David Brown after Aston Martin

After selling Aston Martin, Brown focussed on producing gears, gearboxes, and transmissions for tractors, cars, heavy industry, and the military. His two children, David and Angela, entered the family business and kept it running after his death in 1993. Brown's company continues to produce gears and engine parts.

The V8

The Aston Martin V8 was 250 pounds (113 kg) heavier than its predecessor, thanks to its larger 5.3-liter engine and heavier disk brakes, as well as other improvements. In return for these upgrades, the car had 315 hp, a top speed of 160 mph (257 km/h) and a 0 to 60 acceleration of 5.9 seconds. When Sprague and Minden took over, they decided to build from the V8, creating a **supercharged** variant they called the V8 Vantage.

■ The new V8 model offered a stronger
ZF gearbox, fatter tires, and air conditioning.

Vital Statistics

Aston Martin V8

Production years: 1972–89
(1969–72 as DBS V8)
No. built: 4,021
Top speed: 160 mph (257 km/h)
Engine type: V8
Engine size: 5.3 liters, 315 hp
Cylinders: 8
Transmission: ZF 5-speed manual
all-synchromesh
CO_2 emissions: N/A
EPA fuel economy ratings: N/A
Price: N/A

The Vantage advantage

Unveiled in 1977, the V8 Vantage was hailed as "Britain's First Supercar." Using the 5.3-liter V8 engine of the old V8, but with high-performance **camshafts**, a higher compression ratio, larger inlet valves, and bigger carburetors, the car was faster and more powerful. It was capable of a top speed of 170 mph (274 km/h).

Lagonda luxury

In addition to the Vantage, Aston Martin introduced the Lagonda in 1974. This luxury four-door **sedan** was initially based on the Aston Martin V8, but by 1976 it had been modified to take on a more modern appearance, with a squared-off front grille and straighter lines (a controversial move for Aston Martin enthusiasts, who loved the curves). Although it was eventually named by *Bloomberg Businessweek* as one of the 50 ugliest cars of the last 50 years, it was a groundbreaking experiment. It was the first production car to use a digital instrumentation panel, and had a 280-hp engine capable of pushing the car to a top speed of 149 mph (240 km/h).

Vital Statistics

V8 Vantage

Production years: 1977–89
No. built: 534
Top speed: 170 mph (274 km/h)
Engine type: V8
Engine size: 5.3 liters, 390 hp at 5800 rpm
Cylinders: 8
Transmission: ZF 5-speed manual
CO_2 emissions: N/A
EPA fuel economy ratings: N/A
Price: Approx. US$31,000 (£20,000)

The end of production?

Despite the popularity of the V8 Vantage and the Lagonda, Sprague and Minden found that Aston Martin was taking up too much of their time and finances. Another downturn in the economy in the early 1980s shrank sales to an average of just three cars per week.

The Lagonda was widely regarded as the ugliest Aston Martin ever built.

This forced the owners to think about shutting down production and concentrating just on servicing and restoring older models. Fortunately, a chance meeting between Aston Martin's chairman, Alan Curtis, and a man named Victor Gauntlett provided the company with yet another savior.

The Vantage could do 0 to 60 mph in 5.3 seconds – a tenth of a second faster than the Ferrari Daytona.

Vital Statistics

Lagonda

Production years: 1976–89
No. built: 645
Top speed: 149 mph (240 km/h)
Engine type: V8
Engine size: 5.3 liters, 280 hp
Cylinders: 8
Transmission: 3-speed
   TorqueFlite automatic
CO_2 emissions: N/A
EPA fuel economy ratings: N/A
Price: Approx. US$77,700 (£49,933)

Getting a Gauntlett

Victor Gauntlett was an entrepreneur who had made his money in the British and European oil industry. His shrewd moves during the oil crisis had made him the head of one of Britain's largest oil suppliers—and a very rich man. He was also a car enthusiast, with a special fondness for Bentleys and Aston Martins. When he heard that Aston Martin was in financial trouble, he stepped forward to invest in the company. In 1980, he bought a ten percent stake through his oil company. By 1981, he was fully on board as Aston Martin's executive chairman.

Victor Gauntlett's Aston Martin — on loan to Bond — speeds away from an explosion in the 1987 movie *The Living Daylights.*

Running the Gauntlett

After serving in the Royal Air Force, Gauntlett took his skills and charisma to the oil industry. He gained much of his personal wealth through his own oil company, Hays Petroleum Services. A lover of classic cars, Gauntlett kept racing after leaving Aston Martin, serving as a trustee of the National Motor Museum, U.K. In 1999, he drove a restored Bentley sports car from London to Moscow.

Going global

Gauntlett was a skilled salesman, and he led the sales team in finding new markets for Aston Martin cars. When the Lagonda was named the world's fastest four-seater production car, Gauntlett was able to use the publicity—and his contacts in the oil industry—to sell vehicles in the Middle East, especially oil-rich states such as Qatar, Oman, and Kuwait.

AMAZING FACTS

Gauntlett in the movies?

Although Victor Gauntlett negotiated with the Bond filmmakers about keeping Aston Martin as Bond's car, he turned down an offer to appear in a cameo in *The Living Daylights*, saying he was too busy running the company.

Making changes

It was also Gauntlett who negotiated Aston Martin back into the James Bond film franchise. When the movie producers announced that the next movie, *The Living Daylights*, would return the series to its Sean Connery roots, Gauntlett loaned the them his personal pre-production Vantage.

Gauntlett also wanted to move on from the long-running Aston Martin V8, but knew that this would take time. In the meantime, he brought in revenue by selling the services of his Tickford plant to build parts for other companies' cars. Thus, the Aston Martin interior found its way inside competitor Jaguar's XJS.

Top of the line

While Aston Martin had limited success in producing large numbers of luxury cars for the general market, Gauntlett decided to experiment with supplying cars for the highest of the high end. To do this, he struck a deal with the Italian bodymaker Zagato for a new Aston Martin V8—to be called the V8 Zagato.

This would combine the legendary inner workings of an Aston Martin with the legendary style of a Zagato body. By limiting the number available to the public, Gauntlett gambled, wealthy car enthusiasts would be rushing to buy the cars.

Even at its substantial prices, the V8 Zagato's limited run was sold out before any had been built.

Vital Statistics

V8 Zagato

Production years: 1986–90
No. built: 89
Top speed: 186 mph (300 km/h)
Engine type: V8
Engine size: 5.3 liters, 430 hp
Cylinders: 8
Transmission: ZF 5-speed manual
CO_2 emissions: N/A
EPA fuel economy ratings: N/A
Price: US$156,000

Paying the price

Gauntlett was right. The V8 Zagato was so popular that the company charged £15,000 (around US$22,000) just to add buyers' names to a waiting list. Those at the top of the list had to pay an additional £55,000 (US$80,000) before they got the keys to their car. Most buyers had not even seen the car—they had only looked at a single drawing of what was planned.

Making a fortune

When asked how he could make a small fortune out of running Aston Martin, Gauntlett joked, "Start with a big one." However, he still considered Aston Martin to be a good business interest, saying, "I wouldn't be going into it unless I thought there was money to be made. I am quite convinced there is a niche for a high-quality product. There will always be the people who want the super-duper."

A limited run was launched later in 1986 of an open-top V8 "Volante" edition, 37 of which were produced.

Zagato style

The Zagato was 16 inches (41 cm) shorter than its Vantage predecessor, and ten percent lighter. With a more aerodynamic profile and a 435-hp engine, the V8 Zagato offered top speeds of 186 mph (300 km/h) and a 0–60 acceleration of 4.8 seconds. Instead of the planned 50 cars, Aston Martin actually produced 52, selling the last two for £145,000 (US$235,000).

The profits from the premium production run helped raise funds for the design of a new production car, which would be the company's focus for the remainder of the 1980s. This work would materialize in the form of the Virage, the first new Aston Martin to be unveiled in 20 years.

The Virage

The Virage was intended to be Aston Martin's top model for the 1990s. Although other models introduced during its production run (the DB7 and the new Vantage) offered more powerful engines, the Virage remained the company's most exclusive vehicle. By the time the Virage reached the end of its production life in 2000, 1,050 had been produced.

Aston Martin's heavyweight

The first Virage was unveiled at the Birmingham Motor Show in 1988. Despite its all-aluminum body, it was a heavy vehicle, with a curb weight of nearly 4,000 lb (1,790 kg). However, its 32-valve, 330-hp engine was more than able to keep up. The car boasted a sporty top speed of 158 mph (254 km/h) and could go from 0–60 mph in 6.5 seconds. Critics praised the model: "Acceleration just never seems to run out," said the magazine *Sports Car International*.

The Virage was a hand-built grand tourer, combining the powerful performance of a 5.3-liter V8 engine with a sleek, elegant design and a comfortable interior.

The Volante

At the 1991 Geneva Motor Show, Aston Martin introduced a Volante version of the Virage, a souped-up convertible powered by a 354-hp engine. A year later it would offer a conversion service, allowing Virage owners to upgrade their Aston Martin engines to a 6.3-liter model, boasting 500 hp that was capable of pushing the car to a top speed of 175 mph (282 km/h)—for those times when fast simply wasn't fast enough.

Vital Statistics

Virage

Production years: 1989–2000
No. built: 1,050
Top speed: 158 mph (254 km/h)
Engine type: 32-valve V8
Engine size: 5.3 liters, 315 hp
Cylinders: 8
Transmission: Chrysler 3-speed Torqueflite automatic
CO_2 emissions: N/A
EPA fuel economy ratings: N/A
Price: N/A

➤➤ Financial strain again

Gauntlett's efforts to turn Aston Martin around bore fruit. The company saw its profits rise and its prestige enhanced. It was still in the public eye as the maker of world-famous British luxury automobiles. Despite this, Gauntlett's efforts were a drain on his personal financial resources, and as the oil market tightened in the late 1980s, the costs of keeping Aston Martin growing proved too much for him, and he looked for help elsewhere.

The oil crisis caused problems for car manufacturers in the UK and elsewhere. There were long lines at the pumps for those who could afford the high prices.

Hard times

The 1970s and 1980s were difficult times for most automakers. In 1973, a group of oil-exporting companies in the Middle East increased the price of oil. People could not afford to buy cars that guzzled gas, and governments imposed fuel-efficiency regulations that sports-car makers struggled to meet. The UK's dependence on imported oil, and a tense relationship between industry and labor, led to social problems and political instability.

A chance encounter

Gauntlett's search brought him to the attention of the Ford Motor Company, which was looking to broaden its business with a division of premium luxury automobiles. It was another chance meeting. In May 1987, Gauntlett happened to be staying with other guests at the home of Contessa Maggi, whose husband had founded the Mille Miglia race. There, he met Walter Hayes, vice-president of Ford Motors' European operations. After that meeting, Ford bought a 75 percent share in Aston Martin in September 1987, working in partnership with Gauntlett and helping him finance Aston Martin's re-entry into racing.

Gauntlett bows out

The partnership did not last, however. Possibly, after ten years as the head of Aston Martin, Gauntlett was looking for new challenges. There may have been differences of opinion between Gauntlett and Ford Motors over Aston Martin's entry into racing. Whatever the case, in 1994, Ford bought the remaining shares in Aston Martin, and Gauntlett handed the chairmanship of the company to Hayes.

Despite the success of cars such as the Vantage throughout the 1980s, Gauntlett found running the company too much, and began looking for a buyer for Aston Martin.

Chapter 6

Ford Takes Over »»»»

Aston Martin was now under the control of the American-based Ford Motor Company, absorbed into its Premier Automotive Group. By the time Ford took over in 1994, Aston Martin was at a low ebb. The company had built just 46 cars that year. But its new owner was willing to invest a lot of money into the old company.

Starting over

Several changes were introduced, including mass production rather than the hand-built methods of coachbuilding that Aston Martin had been known for. Ford had also bought Aston Martin's competitor, Jaguar, and decided to combine the talents of the two companies. These moves worried some in the industry. Aston Martin had built its reputation on British handcrafted quality. But under Ford's leadership, production increased. In 1995, Aston Martin produced 700 cars—a company record. And it was again turning heads with its latest model, the DB7.

Vital Statistics

DB7

Production years: 1993–2004
No. built: 7,000
Top speed: 165 mph (266 km/h)
Engine type: Supercharged Inline-6
Engine size: 3.2 liters, 335 hp at 5750 rpm
Cylinders: 6
Transmission: 5-speed manual
CO_2 emissions: N/A
EPA fuel economy ratings: N/A
Price: US$140,000 Coupe; US$150,000 Volante

The DB7 borrowed Jaguar's XJS engine, with a supercharged 3.2-liter straight-six, capable of 335 hp.

Return of the DB

Recalling the classic DB series of cars from the 1950s and 1960s, the DB7 was unveiled at the Geneva Salon in March 1993.

In addition to copying engine designs from Jaguar, Aston Martin borrowed a talented designer by the name of Ian Callum. Having worked as a designer for Ford Motors before joining a small consulting company called TWR Design, Ford commissioned Callum's services for the Aston Martin DB7. He delivered a striking design that rounded out Jaguar's aerodynamic lines into the smoother curves for which Aston Martin was famous.

The DB AR1 was a limited edition grand tourer made for the U.S. market. Only 99 cars were produced, but these sold at the premium price of $226,000. The AR stood for "American Roadster."

DB7 V12 Vantage

Initially intended as an "entry-level" car priced lower than the Virage, the DB7 was an instant hit. By 1998, 2,000 had been built. But Ford didn't stop there. The DB7 V12 Vantage dropped the V6 engine of the DB7 for a powerful all-aluminum 48-valve V12. This produced 400 hp and drove the car to speeds of up to 184 mph (296 km/h), with an acceleration of 0–60 in five seconds. By the time the DB7 was retired (in 2004), 7,000 had been produced—4,458 of them Vantages—which was more than all of the previous DB models combined.

Back to handcrafted

In October 2004, Ford set aside a large part of its plant in Cologne, Germany, for Aston Martin. The new facility could produce up to 5,000 engines per year using 100 specially trained workers. Technicians at Cologne built each engine individually, assembling the parts from start to finish. With each engine taking just under 20 hours to produce, 30 technicians could build enough engines for small runs of high-quality, high-performance vehicles, adjusting each engine to the needs of the client.

The V8 Vantage

As the DB7 model matured, Aston Martin looked ahead to its next project, reintroducing the Vantage. But instead of an updated version of the old grand tourer, the company wanted a leaner and more agile car—something that could compete with the Porsche 911.

A **concept car** called the AMV8 Vantage was unveiled in 2003, and two years later the first production car was introduced. It was a two-door, two-seater made primarily of aluminum to keep the weight down. A 4.3 liter, 32-valve V8 engine provided 380 hp at 7300 rpm, and promised top speeds of 175 mph (282 km/h). The engine featured a unique, racing-style dry-sump lubrication, which allowed the engine to be mounted closer to the ground. This gave the car a lower center of gravity for better handling.

English wheels

A wheeling machine turns a flat sheet of metal into a curved panel that can be used to build a wheel. Metal is placed between a rolling wheel on top and an anvil wheel beneath, and the device presses the wheels together, stretching the metal into a convex shape to make the curve of the wheel, with a *flange* around the edge for strength. Aston Martin still uses this method on its specialty, hand-built cars.

The V8 Vantage was designed to be both elegant and fast.

Vantage roadster

Aston Martin followed up its new Vantage with a souped-up roadster version. Although heavier than the standard model, this convertible boasted the same performance with the same engine.

In 2007, Aston Martin released an upgrade package, allowing owners to pay for upgrades to their Vantage's engine, wheels, and body, including a carbon-fiber **front splitter** and rear wing.

The roadster version of the Vantage had a soft top that could be put up or put away in 18 seconds – while the car was doing speeds of up to 30 mph (48 km/h).

The DB9

Ford invested in a new Aston Martin plant in the tiny town of Gaydon in Warwickshire, England. This was the company's first purpose-built factory, and it immediately began work on the next generation of Aston Martins. The first of these was the DB9.

Ian Callum was again called on to design the body, producing a sleek, wedge-like shape that sliced through the air. Launched in 2003, the DB9 boasted a six-liter V12 engine capable of 470 hp. All of this produced a powerful car capable of a top speed of over 186 mph (300 km/h), which could go from 0–60 mph in 4.8 seconds. Even with its high price tag, Aston Martin could hardly keep up with demand for the DB9.

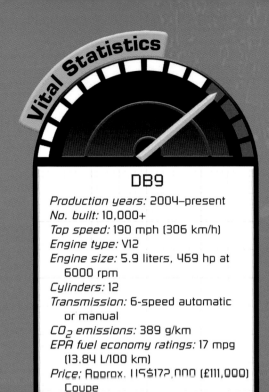

Vital Statistics

DB9

Production years: 2004–present
No. built: 10,000+
Top speed: 190 mph (306 km/h)
Engine type: V12
Engine size: 5.9 liters, 469 hp at 6000 rpm
Cylinders: 12
Transmission: 6-speed automatic or manual
CO_2 emissions: 389 g/km
EPA fuel economy ratings: 17 mpg (13.84 L/100 km)
Price: Approx. US$172,000 (£111,000) Coupe

The DB9 body was made of aluminum that had been specially treated so that the car was light but strong.

← ▪▪

The dashboard of the 2010 DB9.

Back at Newport Pagnell

At its older plant, Aston Martin continued to upgrade its line-up of vehicles, introducing a high-powered V12 car known as the Vanquish.

Unveiled at the 2001 Geneva Motor Show, this was designed by Ian Callum and featured a 450-hp engine able to push the car to a top speed of 185 mph (305 km/h).

AMAZING FACTS

Why no DB8?

To market their new vehicle to the public as a great leap forward from the DB7 in terms of style and design, Aston Martin decided to skip the DB8 entirely and name their new car the DB9.

47

Back to Bond

The Vanquish was praised for its speed and power, but critics disliked the car's semi-**automatic transmission**. When the last 40 Vanquishes were built, Aston Martin offered these models with a fully **manual transmission**, much to the approval of the automotive press. The Vanquish also brought Aston Martin back to the James Bond franchise in *Die Another Day*. Its appearance earned the car third place on *AutoTrader*'s list of Best Film Cars Ever.

The upgraded Vanquish S came with a 514-hp engine and boasted a top speed of 204 mph (328 km/h).

Vital Statistics

Vanquish and Vanquish S

Production years: 2001–07
No. built: 2,587
Top speed: 204 mph (328 km/h)
Engine type: V12
Engine size: 5.9 liters, 450–510 hp at 6500 rpm
Cylinders: 12
Transmission: 6-speed automatic or manual with paddle shifting
CO_2 emissions: N/A
EPA fuel economy ratings: 12 mpg (20 L/100 km) city; 18 mpg (13 L/100 km) highway
Price: N/A

Return to racing

In 2004, Ford decided to bring Aston Martin back to racing, and the company made a deal with the racing engineering group Prodrive, which had been founded in 1984 by a professional racing driver named David Richards. Prodrive's first task was to create a racing version of the DB9. The DBR9 debuted in 2005, featuring an engine block and cylinder heads that were identical to the DB9 road car's V12.

The rest of the car, however, was modified to ensure every last ounce of speed. The DBR9 had a sloped hood and a low profile for aerodynamic performance; carbon fiber was used wherever possible to reduce the car's weight. It was able to accelerate from 0–60 in a heart-stopping 3.4 seconds.

 The DBR9 had a carbon-fiber wing at the back that stopped the car from lifting off the track at high speeds.

Success on the track

The DBR9 won its class in the 12-Hour Sebring race in 2005, and came third at Le Mans. Though it did not win these races, the Aston Martin provided a strong challenge to arch-rival Corvette Racing at many competitions throughout Europe and North America. Aston Martin was a team to be reckoned with.

Chapter 7

A New Era ≫ ≫ ≫ ≫

Between 1991 and 2007, Aston Martin produced over 10,000 vehicles—more than it had built in the 70 previous years. The company was profitable and popular, which was why, as Ford's core business found itself in financial hardship, it looked to sell off the profitable parts of the company. Aston Martin's savior this time was a former racecar driver named David Richards.

The new David Brown?

David Richards graduated university as a chartered accountant, but quickly made his name as a professional racecar driver, winning his first national rally championship in 1974. But his enthusiasm for cars extended beyond the driver's seat. By 1980, he had established new professional races in the Middle East and was managing racing teams for such companies as Porsche and BMW.

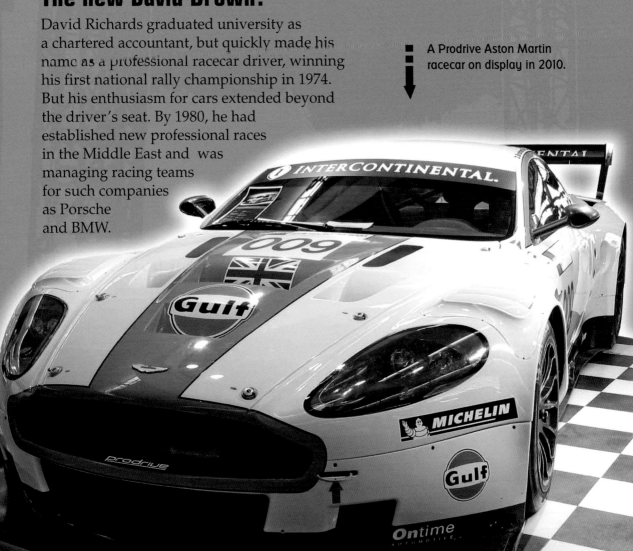

A Prodrive Aston Martin racecar on display in 2010.

Prodrive

In 1984, Richards set up Prodrive, a company to manage motorsports teams in a variety of races, including Formula 1. Prodrive took several automakers to the winners' circle and was paid well for its efforts. This made Richards a wealthy man and, when he learned that Aston Martin was up for sale, he organized the group of investors to buy the company and became chairman.

Richards wanted to buy Aston Martin because he loved the brand and its racing pedigree. But while the purchase may have been motivated by a love of the brand, Richards was still a smart businessman who threw himself into the operation of what was already a profitable company. He was also willing to move away from Aston Martin's British heritage.

▲ Ulrich Bez outside the Gaydon plant. In 2011, he announced plans to start exporting Aston Martins to China.

Expanding to Europe and the world

Richards made German-born Ulrich Bez Chief Executive Officer of Aston Martin. Bez had actually been Aston Martin's CEO since 2000 under Ford's ownership, but Richards saw in Bez a strong leader who could help him take the company forward.

Ulrich Bez

Bez studied engineering and began a career in automobile design. He was responsible for the development of cars including Porsche's 911 Turbo, BMW's Z1 and the Daewoo Matiz. He became the CEO and chairman of Aston Martin in 2000, and helped develop the DB9 and Vantage. Bez drove an Aston Martin Vantage in the 24-Hours Nurburgring endurance race from 2006 to 2008.

Production shifts

Production moved from Newport Pagnell to the Gaydon plant, and a deal was struck with Austrian automaker Magna Steyr to build up to 2,000 Aston Martins at Graz, Austria. Indeed, Aston Martin's board has speculated on moving all of Aston Martin's operations—except marketing—from Britain to Europe.

Richards believed that Aston Martin could not survive by simply being a British automaker building a British car. Since he took over, Aston Martin has opened more dealerships in Europe, and its first branches in China. Aston Martin now has over 120 dealers operating in 28 countries.

The new Vantage and DB9

Bez set to work upgrading two models that were in production at the time Richards took over. The V8 Vantage had its 4.3-liter engine upgraded to 4.7-liter, capable of 420 hp. At the same time, a V12 version was unveiled, featuring a 510-hp, six-liter engine capable of pushing the car to speeds of 190 mph (310 km/h). Planned production of the V12 is already above 1,000 units, with sales expected across the world. For the DB9, a more powerful engine was installed in 2008, along with a redesigned interior.

Aston Martins roll off the production line at the Gaydon plant in 2008.

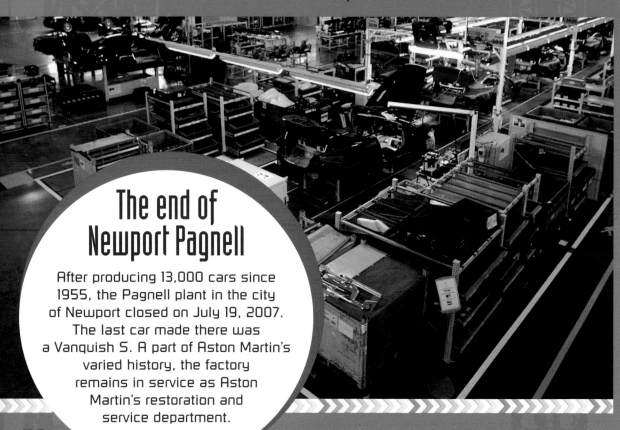

The end of Newport Pagnell

After producing 13,000 cars since 1955, the Pagnell plant in the city of Newport closed on July 19, 2007. The last car made there was a Vanquish S. A part of Aston Martin's varied history, the factory remains in service as Aston Martin's restoration and service department.

The new DBS

Finally, for its top-of-the-line model, Aston Martin unveiled the new DBS. Boasting a six-liter V12 engine capable of 510 hp, the DBS could reach speeds of 191 mph (307 km/h). This premium vehicle again brought Aston Martin back to the silver screen, appearing in the 2006 James Bond movie, *Casino Royale*. Buyers flooded in, buying out the entire production for the next five years before the first car even rolled off the line.

Vital Statistics

Vantage V12

Production years: 2007–present
No. built: 1,500+
Top speed: 190 mph (306 km/h)
Engine type: V12
Engine size: 6.0 liters, 510 hp
Cylinders: 12
Transmission: 6-speed manual or semi-automatic
CO_2 emissions: N/A
EPA fuel economy ratings: 12 mpg (19.6 L/100 km) city; 19 mpg (12.38 L/100 km) highway
Price: US$209,000

The DBS V12 Volante was introduced in 2007. So far, more than 1,500 have been built.

53

Back to the track

With professional racer David Richards in control of the company, it was no surprise to see Aston Martin increase its participation in organized racing. In January 2009, Aston Martin Racing announced that it would field a factory team in the 24 Hours of Le Mans race. It would use a specially built Le Mans Prototype (a special class of racing vehicle capable of speeds faster than a Formula 1 racecar) co-developed by Aston Martin and the British racing company Lola Cars. The name of the car was the DBR1-2, recalling the DBR1 chassis that won six races in 1959, including that year's Le Mans.

The Le Mans series DBR9 brought Aston Martin back to the racetrack in 2009.

The DBR1-2

The DBR1-2 used a six-liter V12 engine from a DBR9, adding larger air restrictors to increase horsepower. A more compact Xtrac six-speed gearbox replaced the standard Lola version. In total, three Lola-Aston Martins were built for entry in the Le Mans race.

Success at Le Mans

Despite a shaky start in the pre-season, when one of the cars (numbered 007, possibly winking at Aston Martin's James Bond connection) was destroyed in an accident, Aston Martin rebuilt the car and raced all three at Le Mans in 2009. The rebuilt car completed 373 laps in 24 hours, finishing fourth overall and fourth in its class. The other two cars also fared well, completing 342 laps and 252 laps respectively. Based on the way Le Mans awarded points, Lola-Aston Martin 007 won the Le Mans Series overall, while car 009 finished fourth.

A century on

It is almost 100 years since Lionel Martin and Robert Bamford unveiled the first Aston Martin. Since then, the company has changed ownership several times. It has faced bankruptcy at least four times, and it has produced over 44,000 cars, more than 32,000 of those in the last 20 years. Like James Bond, Aston Martin cars are suave and sophisticated, but have a heart of steel.

The Lola-Aston Martin 009 was one of three vehicles raced at the 2009 Le Mans event. It came fourth.

Aston Martin today and tomorrow

Under the leadership of Richards and Bez, Aston Martin is profitable and developing impressive new models. One of these, the Aston Martin One-77, was unveiled at the Paris Motor Show in 2008. This model, planned for a limited run of only 77 cars, features a full carbon-fiber chassis, an aluminum body sculpted by hand, and a super-powerful 750-hp, 7.3-liter V12 engine. A test drive in December 2009 showed that the car had a top speed of 220 mph (354 km/h) and a 0–60 acceleration of 3.5 seconds.

Vital Statistics

Aston Martin One-77

Production years: 2011–12
No. built: 77
Top speed: 220 mph (354 km/h)
Engine type: V12 with dry sump lubrication
Engine size: 6.0 liters, 750 hp
Cylinders: 12
Transmission: 6-speed automatic
CO_2 *emissions:* N/A
EPA fuel economy ratings: N/A
Price: Approx. US$1,065,000 (£1,200,000)

■■➡

The One-77 hasn't been made available for sale yet, but its limited run will command top prices. The model is expected to sell out.

ONE-77

The Virage and the Rapide

For the more standard production cars, Aston Martin has unveiled the four-door Rapide and relaunched the Virage to sell alongside its DB9 and DBS models. The Virage, available in a two-door coupe or volante, will offer a 490-hp V12 engine capable of 0–60 mph acceleration in less than five seconds. The Rapide has a 470-hp V12 engine and promises a top speed of 188 mph (303 km/h).

The Rapide can do 0–60 mph in 5.1 seconds. Aston Martin is already producing 1,250 Rapides per year.

Vital Statistics

Rapide

Production years: 2010–present
No. built: N/A
Top speed: 188 mph (302 km/h)
Engine type: V12
Engine size: 6.0 liters, 470 hp
Cylinders: 12
Transmission: Touchtronic 2 6-speed automatic
CO_2 emissions: N/A
EPA fuel economy ratings: N/A
Price: US$199,950 (£139,950)

» Tradition meets technology

Aston Martin built its reputation by building its cars to be powerful, fast, and luxurious, emphasizing the craftsmanship of its manufacturer. While the company cherishes its heritage, it has not been afraid to embrace the newest technology if it makes the cars lighter, faster, more powerful, or a better all-round experience for the driver.

Aston Martin was the first to feature a digital instrument display, so you can expect that as new technologies materialize, they will be added to the latest models.

■ The new Virage is available in V8 and V12 models. The V12 has a top speed of 186 mph (299 km/h) and can do 0–60 in 4.6 seconds.

Aston Martin v. Ferrari

Ulrich Bez has said: "In many ways, Ferrari is a mass-market brand. It is a very public brand and it is 'owned' by Italy ... Aston Martin is respected, but the people do not feel that they own it. Ferrari has developed perfumes and lots of mass-market things ... The visibility and image are not positive. That is my opinion."

58

The way forward

For David Richards, the best way forward for Aston Martin was to take the best of its history, and marry it to the most promising new technologies, new production methods and new markets. In this way, Aston Martin's development has mirrored that of Britain. Even as the countries of Europe drew closer together, Britain was protective of its independence, but it still reached out in partnership for a bigger place on the world stage.

Aston Martin's CEO Ulrich Bez is quoted as saying that the heart of British tradition is not a particular car or institution, it is discipline.

For Aston Martin, competing on the world stage means actually working throughout it, embracing that flare and creativity in a disciplined way that is the heart of the company's British character.

■
After nearly 100 years, Aston Martin looks set to continue setting records on and off the racetrack.

Aston Martin Timeline

1913   Bamford & Martin Ltd. is founded

1915   The first Aston Martin car is built, but World War I halts production

1921   Production starts on the Standard Sports Series

1922   The "Green Pea" races in the French Grand Prix; Martin buys out Bamford

1924   Aston Martin declares bankruptcy

1926   Lionel leaves Aston Martin; Bertelli and Renwick take over

1927   Bertelli's First Series begins production

1934   Le Mans Mark II is introduced; the "Ulsters" make a clean sweep at Goodwood

1936   Bertelli quits Aston Martin

1947   David Brown buys Aston Martin

1948   The Atom wins the Spa 24-Hour race; the "Spa Replica" and DB1 debut at the London Motor Show

1950   The DB2 is unveiled

1958   Launch of the DB4

1959   DBR1 racecar wins Le Mans and is named World Sportscar of the Year; *Goldfinger* is published, starting the association between Aston Martin and James Bond

1963   The DB4 Vantage is upgraded to the DB5

1967   A larger coupe version of the DB6, the DBS, goes on sale

1972   David Brown leaves; the eight-cylinder DBS is revamped as the Aston Martin V8

1974   The Lagonda is launched

1977   The V8 Vantage is hailed as "Britain's First Supercar"

1980   Victor Gauntlett buys into Aston Martin

1986   The high-end V8 Zagato is introduced

1989   Production begins on the Virage

1993   The DB7 is unveiled at the Geneva Salon

1994   Ford takes full control of Aston Martin

2000   Ulrich Bez joins Aston Martin

2001   The Ian Callum-designed Vanquish makes its debut

2004   Launch of the DB9; Aston Martin returns to racing, making a deal with Prodrive

2005   The DBR9 makes an impression on the circuit; Vantage V8 and V12 go on sale

2006   Ford sells Aston Martin; ex-racing driver David Richards takes over; the new DBS makes its movie debut in *Casino Royale*

2009   Aston Martin goes back to Le Mans with three DBR1-2s

2011   The Aston Martin One-77 is unveiled

Further Information

Books

Aston Martin: A Racing History
by Anthony Pritchard
(Haynes Publishing, 2006)

British Auto Legends: Classics of Style and Design
by Michael Zumbrunn and Richard Heseltine
(Merrell, 2007)

Original Aston Martin DB4/5/6
by Robert Edwards, Martyn Goddard, and Mark Hughes.
(Bay View, 1992)

Websites

www.astonmartin.com/
Aston Martin's official website

www.astonmartinracing.com/
Official Aston Martin Racing website

www.amoc.org/
Aston Martin Owners Club

http://designmuseum.org/design/aston-martin
Great British Design Quest: Aston Martin

www.amlvantage.com/
North American Aston Martin Showcase (fan site)

http://sprague.com/blog/?page_id=3
Peter Sprague's recollections of his time at Aston Martin

Glossary

acceleration A measure of how quickly something speeds up

aerodynamic Describing something with a low amount of drag

automatic transmission A device that shifts a car's gears without help from the driver according to the speed it is traveling

bankruptcy When a company or individual runs out of money

brake horsepower (bhp) The raw horsepower of an engine before the loss of power caused by the alternator, gearbox, differential, pumps, etc.

camshaft A rod in a car's engine; as the camshaft turns, it pushes the pistons up and down, compressing gas in the engine and powering the car

carburetors Devices in engines that mix the fuel and air

chassis The strong support structure that connects the engine to the wheels and holds the body to the car

concept car A vehicle made to show the public a new design or technology

coupe A hard-topped sports car with two doors

cylinder head A detatchable metal casing on an engine cylinder, which contains part of the combustion chamber

flagship The most important or successful model in a series

flange A rim that sticks out over the edge of a wheel, which makes it stronger or holds it in place

front splitter A device attached to the front of a car that reduces drag

grand tourer A sports car that is made for driving long distances

Great Depression A period in the 1930s when the world economy went into decline

horsepower (hp) The amount of pulling power an engine has based on the number of horses it would take to pull the same load

iconic Something that is much loved and admired

manual transmission A device that a driver must operate to shift a car's gears

modified When something is altered so that it suits a particular purpose

patron Someone who supports or sponsors someone or something

pedigree Something or someone's origins, history, and ancestors

prestige The respect with which someone or something is regarded by other people

production cars Cars that are made in large numbers on an assembly line

prototype The original or test version of a car, which is later modified and developed into a production car

roadster A two-seater car with a soft-top roof; also known as a spyder

sedan A passenger car with four doors and a back seat

streamlined Something that is designed to have the least resistance to the flow of air

supercharged When an air compressor is used for the forced induction of an internal combustion engine

synchromesh A system for shifting gears that allows them to revolve at the same speed, so that they can be shifted smoothly

transmission The device in a car that allows the driver to change gears

wheelbase The distance between the front and rear wheels in a car

Index

Entries in **bold** indicate pictures